Mastering Smartsheet: Unleashing the Power of Project Management and Collaboration

Chapter 4: Organizing Data with Filters and Views

Filtering data for better organization

Creating and managing different views

Utilizing reports for data analysis

Chapter 5: Collaborating in Smartsheet

Sharing sheets and collaborating with team members

Setting permissions and access levels

Communicating within Smartsheet

Chapter 6: Task Management and Project Planning

Creating and managing tasks

Building project timelines and schedules

Assigning resources and dependencies

Chapter 7: Automating Workflows with Automations

Introduction to Automations

Chapter 1: Introduction to Smartsheet

Welcome to the world of Smartsheet! In this chapter, we'll introduce you to the basics of Smartsheet, including its history, core features, and how to get started using it.

1.1 Overview of Smartsheet

Smartsheet is a powerful platform that combines the familiar interface of a spreadsheet with robust project management functionalities. It allows individuals and teams to collaborate, organize, and manage projects more efficiently. Whether you're tracking tasks, creating project timelines, or managing resources, Smartsheet provides the tools you need to stay organized and productive.

1.2 Brief History and Evolution

Originally founded in 2005, Smartsheet has evolved from a simple spreadsheet tool to a comprehensive work management platform used by millions of users worldwide. Over the years, it has continuously added new features and capabilities to meet the evolving needs of businesses and teams across various industries.

1.3 Core Features and Functionalities

Here are some of the key features that make Smartsheet a valuable tool for project management and collaboration:

- Sheets:

Sheets are the foundation of Smartsheet. They resemble traditional spreadsheets, allowing you to organize data in rows and columns. However, Smartsheet goes beyond basic spreadsheets by offering additional functionalities such as attachments, comments, and task assignments.

- Rows and Columns:

Rows and columns are used to structure data within sheets. You can customize columns to suit your specific needs, whether it's tracking dates, assigning priorities, or capturing status updates. Rows represent individual items or tasks within your project.

- Collaboration:

Smartsheet facilitates collaboration among team members by allowing them to share sheets, comment on tasks, and communicate in real-time. With features like @mentions and notifications, it's easy to keep everyone on the same page.

- Project Management:

Smartsheet offers robust project management capabilities, including task tracking, Gantt charts, and resource management. You can create project timelines, assign tasks to team members, and monitor progress in real-time.

1.4 Getting Started with Smartsheet
Now that you have an overview of Smartsheet, let's dive into how you can get started using it.

- Sign Up for an Account:

Visit the Smartsheet website and sign up for an account. You can choose from various subscription plans based on your needs, including individual, team, and enterprise options.

- Explore the Interface:

Once you've signed up, take some time to explore the Smartsheet interface. Familiarize yourself with the different components, such as sheets, rows, and columns. You can also customize your workspace to suit your preferences.

- Access Help Resources:

Smartsheet offers a wealth of resources to help you learn and navigate the platform. Take advantage of tutorials, help articles, and video guides to enhance your understanding of Smartsheet's features and functionalities.

Congratulations! You've completed the first chapter of our Smartsheet tutorial. In the next chapter, we'll delve deeper into creating and customizing sheets. Get ready to unleash the full potential of Smartsheet for your projects!

Chapter 2: Getting Started with Smartsheet

In this chapter, we'll dive deeper into using Smartsheet by learning how to create and customize sheets, import data, and navigate the interface effectively.

2.1 Creating a New Sheet

To create a new sheet in Smartsheet, follow these steps:

Navigate to the Sheets List: Once you're logged in to your Smartsheet account, you'll see the Sheets List, which displays all your existing sheets. Click on the "+" icon or the "New" button to create a new sheet.

Choose a Template (Optional): Smartsheet offers various templates for common use cases such as project management, task tracking, and budgeting. You can choose a template that fits your needs or start with a blank sheet.

Name Your Sheet: Give your new sheet a descriptive name that reflects its purpose or content.

Set Up Columns: Define the columns for your sheet by clicking on the "+" icon next to "Add column" or by selecting a predefined set of columns based on the template you chose.

Customize Column Properties (Optional): Depending on your requirements, you can customize the properties of each column, such as the data type (text, date, dropdown), format, and validation rules.

Add Rows: Once your columns are set up, you can start adding rows to your sheet. Each row represents an individual item or task within your project.

Fill in Data: Enter the relevant data into each cell of your sheet. You can type directly into the cells or copy and paste data from another source.

2.2 Importing Data

If you have existing data that you'd like to bring into Smartsheet, you can import it from various sources, including Excel spreadsheets, Google Sheets, and CSV files. Here's how:

Open a Sheet: Navigate to the sheet where you want to import data or create a new sheet if needed.

Go to the Import Data Option: Look for the "File" menu at the top left corner of the Smartsheet interface. From there, select "Import Data" and choose the source from which you want to import.

Map Columns (if required): Smartsheet will prompt you to map the columns in your source file to the columns in your sheet. This ensures that the data is imported correctly and matches the structure of your sheet.

Review and Confirm: Once you've mapped the columns, review the imported data to ensure accuracy. Make any necessary adjustments and confirm the import.

2.3 Navigating the Interface

To navigate the Smartsheet interface effectively, familiarize yourself with the following key components:

Sheets List: Displays all your sheets and allows you to navigate between them.

Toolbar: Contains various tools and options for working with sheets, including formatting, sharing, and printing.

Sheet Tabs: If you have multiple sheets open, you can switch between them using the sheet tabs at the bottom of the interface.

Workspace: The main area where you'll work with your sheets. Here, you can view and edit data, apply filters, and perform other actions.

By mastering these basic skills, you'll be well on your way to harnessing the full potential of Smartsheet for your projects. In the next chapter, we'll explore how to customize sheets and tailor them to your specific needs.

Chapter 3: Creating and Customizing Sheets

In this chapter, we'll delve into the process of creating and customizing sheets in Smartsheet to tailor them to your specific project needs.

3.1 Creating a New Sheet

To create a new sheet in Smartsheet, follow these steps:

Navigate to the Sheets List: Log in to your Smartsheet account and access the Sheets List by clicking on the grid icon located in the top left corner of the interface.

Click on the "+" Icon: In the Sheets List, you'll find a "+" icon or a "New" button. Click on it to initiate the creation of a new sheet.

Choose a Template (Optional): Smartsheet offers a variety of templates tailored for different purposes, such as project management, task tracking, and budgeting. You can either choose a template or start with a blank sheet.

Name Your Sheet: Give your sheet a descriptive name that reflects its purpose or content. This will help you and your team members easily identify it.

Set Up Columns: Define the columns for your sheet based on the type of data you need to track. You can add columns by clicking on the "+" icon next to "Add column" or selecting predefined sets of columns based on the template chosen.

Customize Column Properties (Optional): Depending on your requirements, you can customize the properties of each column, such as the data type (text, date, dropdown), format, and validation rules.

Add Rows: Once your columns are set up, you can start adding rows to your sheet. Each row represents an individual item or task within your project.

Fill in Data: Enter the relevant data into each cell of your sheet. You can type directly into the cells or copy and paste data from another source.

3.2 Customizing Columns

Smartsheet allows you to customize columns to suit your specific needs. Here's how you can customize columns:

Hover over the Column Header: Move your cursor over the header of the column you want to customize.

Click on the Dropdown Arrow: A dropdown arrow will appear next to the column header. Click on it to reveal a menu of customization options.

Select "Edit Column Properties": From the dropdown menu, choose the "Edit Column Properties" option.

Customize Properties: In the Column Properties dialog box, you can customize various properties of the column, such as the column name, data type, format, and validation rules.

Save Changes: Once you've made your desired changes, click on the "Save" button to apply them.

3.3 Using Conditional Formatting

Conditional formatting allows you to visually highlight cells based on specific criteria. Here's how you can use conditional formatting in Smartsheet:

Select Cells: Click and drag to select the cells you want to apply conditional formatting to.

Open the Formatting Menu: Right-click on the selected cells and choose the "Format" option from the context menu, or click on the "Format" icon in the toolbar.

Choose Conditional Formatting: In the Formatting menu, select the "Conditional Formatting" tab.

Set Conditions: Click on the "Add" button to define conditions for formatting. You can specify criteria such as text contains, date is before, or number is greater than.

Choose Formatting Options: Once you've set the conditions, choose the formatting options you want to apply to cells that meet those conditions, such as text color, background color, or font style.

Apply Formatting: Click on the "Apply" button to apply the conditional formatting to the selected cells.

By following these steps, you can create and customize sheets in Smartsheet to effectively track and manage your projects. In the next chapter, we'll explore how to organize data using filters and views.

Chapter 4: Organizing Data with Filters and Views

In this chapter, we'll explore how to organize and visualize your data effectively in Smartsheet using filters and views.

4.1 Filtering Data

Filters allow you to narrow down the data displayed on your sheet based on specific criteria. Here's how to use filters in Smartsheet:

Select the Range: Click on any cell within the range of data you want to filter.

Open the Filter Menu: In the toolbar, locate the filter icon (it looks like a funnel) and click on it to open the filter menu.

Add Filter Criteria: In the filter menu, you can add multiple criteria to filter your data. Choose the column you want to filter by, specify the condition (e.g., equals, contains, greater than), and enter the value you want to filter by.

Apply Filters: Once you've set your filter criteria, click on the "Apply" button to apply the filters to your sheet. Only the rows that meet the specified criteria will be displayed.

Clear Filters: To remove filters and display all the data again, click on the filter icon in the toolbar and choose the "Clear" option.

4.2 Creating and Managing Views

Views allow you to save different configurations of your sheet, including filter settings, column visibility, and sort order. Here's how to create and manage views in Smartsheet:

Set Up Your Sheet: Customize your sheet with the desired filter settings, column visibility, and sort order.

Save the View: In the toolbar, click on the "Views" menu and select "Save View." Give your view a descriptive name and click "Save." This will save the current configuration of your sheet as a new view.

Switch Between Views: To switch between views, click on the "Views" menu and select the view you want to switch to. Smartsheet will instantly apply the saved configuration to your sheet.

Edit or Delete Views: To edit or delete views, click on the "Views" menu and choose "Manage Views." From there, you can rename, edit, or delete existing views as needed.

4.3 Utilizing Reports for Data Analysis

Reports in Smartsheet allow you to consolidate data from multiple sheets and visualize it in a single location. Here's how to create and utilize reports:

Create a Report: In the toolbar, click on the "Reports" menu and select "New Report." Choose the sheets you want to include in the report and specify the columns you want to display.

Customize Report Settings: Customize the settings of your report, such as grouping and sorting options, summary fields, and filters.

View and Analyze Data: Once your report is created, you can view and analyze the consolidated data from multiple sheets. You can also apply filters and drill down into specific details as needed.

Share and Collaborate: Share your report with team members to collaborate and make data-driven decisions together. You can also schedule automatic updates to keep the report data current.

By mastering filters, views, and reports, you can organize and analyze your data effectively in Smartsheet, gaining valuable insights to drive your projects forward. In the next chapter, we'll explore collaboration features in Smartsheet and how to work effectively with your team members.

Chapter 5: Collaborating in Smartsheet

In this chapter, we'll explore the collaboration features in Smartsheet and how to work effectively with your team members.

5.1 Sharing Sheets

Sharing sheets in Smartsheet allows you to collaborate with team members, clients, and stakeholders. Here's how to share a sheet:

Open the Sheet: Navigate to the sheet you want to share.

Click on the Share Button: In the toolbar, click on the "Share" button. This will open the sharing options menu.

Add Collaborators: Enter the email addresses of the individuals you want to share the sheet with. You can also specify their access level, such as Editor, Viewer, or Admin.

Customize Sharing Settings (Optional): You can customize additional sharing settings, such as allowing collaborators to edit, comment, or view attachments. You can also set permissions for specific rows or columns if needed.

Send Invitations: Once you've configured the sharing settings, click on the "Send" button to send invitations to the collaborators. They will receive an email notification with a link to access the shared sheet.

5.2 Collaborating in Real-Time

Smartsheet enables real-time collaboration, allowing team members to work together on the same sheet simultaneously. Here's how it works:

Multiple Users Editing: When multiple users are editing the same sheet at the same time, their changes are automatically synced in real-time. You can see the changes made by other users as they happen.

Comments and Discussions: Use the comments feature to leave feedback, ask questions, and discuss specific aspects of the sheet. You can mention specific collaborators using "@mentions" to notify them about the comment.

Activity Log: The activity log tracks all changes made to the sheet, including who made the changes and when. You can access the activity log to review the history of edits and track the progress of your team members.

5.3 Setting Permissions and Access Levels

Smartsheet allows you to control access to your sheets by setting permissions and access levels for collaborators. Here's how to do it:

Access Levels: Smartsheet offers three access levels: Editor, Viewer, and Admin. Editors can make changes to the sheet, viewers can only view the sheet without editing, and admins have full control over sharing settings.

Row and Column Permissions: You can also set permissions for specific rows and columns within the sheet. This allows you to restrict access to sensitive information or limit editing rights to certain sections of the sheet.

Sharing Options: In addition to individual sharing, you can also share sheets with entire groups or domains. This makes it easy to collaborate with teams and departments within your organization.

5.4 Communicating Within Smartsheet

Smartsheet offers built-in communication tools to facilitate collaboration and streamline communication within your team. Here are some key features:

Notifications: Smartsheet sends notifications to collaborators when they are mentioned in comments, assigned tasks, or when changes are made to the sheet.

Alerts and Reminders: You can set up alerts and reminders to notify team members about approaching deadlines, overdue tasks, or other important events.

Update Requests: Use update requests to gather status updates from team members. You can send requests for specific information and track responses directly within Smartsheet.

By leveraging these collaboration features, you can work more efficiently with your team members, share information securely, and keep everyone aligned towards common goals. In the next chapter, we'll explore task management and project planning in Smartsheet.

Chapter 6: Task Management and Project Planning

In this chapter, we'll delve into the robust task management and project planning capabilities of Smartsheet, enabling you to efficiently organize, assign, and track tasks within your projects.

6.1 Creating Tasks

Tasks are the building blocks of projects in Smartsheet. Here's how to create tasks:

Open the Sheet: Navigate to the sheet where you want to create tasks, or create a new sheet specifically for task management.

Add a Task Row: Click on an empty row in the sheet to add a new task. You can also use the shortcut key "Ctrl + Shift + R" to insert a new row.

Enter Task Details: In the task row, enter the details of the task, such as the task name, description, assignee, start date, due date, priority, and any other relevant information.

Customize Task Columns (Optional): Customize the columns in your sheet to include additional information specific to your project, such as task status, dependencies, estimated effort, and more.

Repeat for Additional Tasks: Repeat the process to add additional tasks to your sheet until all tasks for your project are listed.

6.2 Building Project Timelines and Schedules

Smartsheet offers powerful tools for building project timelines and schedules, including Gantt charts and dependencies. Here's how to do it:

Enable the Gantt View: Click on the "View" menu in the toolbar and select "Gantt Chart" to enable the Gantt view for your sheet.
Set Up Dependencies: Use dependencies to define the relationships between tasks. Click on a task in the Gantt chart, drag the dependency arrow to another task, and release to create a dependency.

Adjust Task Dates: Drag and drop tasks in the Gantt chart to adjust their start and end dates. Smartsheet will automatically update the task durations and dependencies accordingly.

Customize Gantt Chart Options: Customize the appearance of your Gantt chart by adjusting options such as date range, timeline scale, bar styles, and more.
Share Gantt Chart: Share your Gantt chart with team members and stakeholders to communicate project timelines and milestones effectively.

6.3 Assigning Resources and Dependencies

Assigning resources and managing task dependencies are essential aspects of project planning. Here's how to do it in Smartsheet:

Assigning Resources: Use the "Assigned To" column to assign tasks to specific team members. You can assign tasks to individuals or groups, depending on your project's needs.

Managing Dependencies: Use dependencies to define the logical relationships between tasks. You can set dependencies such as "Finish-to-Start," "Start-to-Start," "Finish-to-Finish," or "Start-to-Finish" to specify how tasks are related to each other.

Visualizing Dependencies: Dependencies are visually represented in the Gantt chart, allowing you to see how changes to one task affect the schedule of dependent tasks.

Resolving Conflicts: Smartsheet automatically identifies and highlights conflicts between task dependencies, helping you identify potential scheduling issues and resolve them proactively.

By leveraging these task management and project planning features in Smartsheet, you can create comprehensive project schedules, allocate resources effectively, and ensure smooth project execution. In the next chapter, we'll explore advanced automation capabilities in Smartsheet to streamline your workflow further.

Chapter 7: Automating Workflows with Automations

In this chapter, we'll explore the powerful automation capabilities of Smartsheet, allowing you to streamline repetitive tasks, increase efficiency, and reduce manual effort.

7.1 Introduction to Automations

Automations in Smartsheet enable you to automate various actions and workflows based on predefined triggers and conditions. Here's an overview of the key concepts:

Triggers: Triggers are events that initiate automation actions. Examples of triggers include when a new row is added, when a specific cell is updated, or when a certain condition is met.

Actions: Actions are the tasks that you want Smartsheet to perform automatically in response to a trigger. Actions can include sending notifications, updating cells, creating new rows, and more.

Conditions: Conditions allow you to specify criteria that must be met for an automation action to be triggered. For example, you can create a condition to only send a notification when a task is overdue.

7.2 Setting Up Automated Actions

Here's how to set up automated actions in Smartsheet:

Access Automations: In your sheet, click on the "Automation" menu in the toolbar and select "Manage Automations" to access the automation settings.

Create New Automation: Click on the "New Automation" button to create a new automation rule.

Define Trigger: Choose the trigger that will initiate the automation action. This could be a specific event such as a cell value change, a date-based trigger, or a manual trigger.

Set Conditions (Optional): If you want the automation action to be triggered only under certain conditions, define the conditions accordingly.

Specify Action: Choose the action you want Smartsheet to perform when the trigger is activated. This could include sending notifications, updating cells, creating new rows, or executing a webhook.

Configure Action Settings: Customize the settings of the chosen action, such as recipient email addresses for notifications or the content of cell updates.

Save Automation: Once you've configured the trigger and action settings, save the automation rule to activate it.

7.3 Examples of Automation Use Cases
Here are some common examples of how you can use automations in Smartsheet to streamline your workflows:

Notification Alerts: Set up notifications to alert team members when tasks are assigned to them, deadlines are approaching, or changes are made to critical data.

Task Assignment: Automatically assign tasks to team members based on specific criteria, such as workload capacity or expertise.

Status Updates: Update the status of tasks automatically based on predefined conditions, such as completion of dependent tasks or reaching a certain milestone.

Data Synchronization: Sync data between Smartsheet and other applications or databases using webhooks or API integrations.

Approval Workflows: Set up automated approval workflows to route documents or requests to the appropriate stakeholders for review and approval.

By leveraging automations effectively, you can save time, reduce errors, and increase productivity in your projects and workflows. In the next chapter, we'll explore advanced formulas and functions in Smartsheet for more advanced data manipulation and analysis.

Chapter 8: Advanced Formulas and Functions

In this chapter, we'll delve into advanced formulas and functions in Smartsheet, empowering you to perform complex calculations, manipulate data, and enhance your project management capabilities.

8.1 Exploring Smartsheet Functions

Smartsheet offers a wide range of functions to perform calculations, manipulate data, and automate tasks. Here are some key functions you should be familiar with:

SUM: Adds up the values in a range of cells.

IF: Returns one value if a condition is true and another value if it's false.

VLOOKUP: Searches for a value in the first column of a range and returns a value in the same row from another column.

DATE: Returns the current date or constructs a date from year, month, and day components.

COUNTIF: Counts the number of cells that meet a specific condition.

8.2 Using Formulas for Data Analysis

Formulas in Smartsheet can be used for various data analysis tasks, such as calculating totals, averages, percentages, and more. Here's how to use formulas for data analysis:

Enter Formula: Click on the cell where you want the result of the formula to appear and start typing the formula directly into the cell.

Reference Cells: Use cell references to include values from other cells in your formula. You can reference individual cells, ranges of cells, or named ranges.

Apply Functions: Use built-in functions to perform calculations and manipulate data within your formula. You can combine multiple functions to create more complex calculations.

Review Results: Once you've entered the formula, Smartsheet will automatically calculate the result and display it in the cell. Review the result to ensure it matches your expectations.

8.3 Creating Complex Formulas

In addition to basic arithmetic operations, Smartsheet allows you to create complex formulas to handle more sophisticated calculations. Here are some advanced formula techniques you can use:

Nested Functions: Combine multiple functions within a single formula to perform more complex calculations. You can nest functions inside each other to create intricate formulas.

Logical Functions: Use logical functions such as IF, AND, and OR to create conditional calculations based on specific criteria.

Error Handling: Use functions like IFERROR to handle errors gracefully and display custom messages or values in case of errors.

Array Formulas: Use array formulas to perform calculations on multiple cells at once and return multiple results in a single formula.

8.4 Applying Formulas to Project Management

Formulas can be particularly useful for project management tasks in Smartsheet. Here are some examples of how you can apply formulas to project management:

Calculate Task Durations: Use formulas to calculate the duration of tasks based on start and end dates, taking into account weekends and holidays.

Track Budgets and Expenses: Use formulas to calculate total project costs, track expenses against budgets, and generate financial reports.

Automate Status Updates: Use formulas to automatically update task statuses based on predefined criteria, such as completion percentage or deadline status.

Generate Dynamic Reports: Use formulas to aggregate and summarize project data dynamically, allowing you to create interactive reports that update automatically as the project progresses.

By mastering advanced formulas and functions in Smartsheet, you can unlock new possibilities for data analysis, automation, and project management. In the next chapter, we'll explore how to integrate Smartsheet with other tools to enhance your productivity further.

Chapter 9: Integrating Smartsheet with Other Tools

In this chapter, we'll explore how to integrate Smartsheet with other tools to enhance your productivity, streamline workflows, and centralize data management.

9.1 Integration with Microsoft Office

Smartsheet offers seamless integration with Microsoft Office applications, allowing you to work more efficiently with familiar tools like Excel, Word, and Outlook. Here's how to integrate Smartsheet with Microsoft Office:

Excel Integration: Import data from Excel into Smartsheet or export Smartsheet data to Excel for further analysis. You can also create live connections between Smartsheet and Excel for real-time data syncing.

Word Integration: Use Smartsheet Merge for Word to create customized documents, reports, and letters using data from Smartsheet. Merge data directly from Smartsheet into Word templates to streamline document creation.

Outlook Integration: Add Smartsheet as an Outlook add-in to easily create tasks, assignees, and due dates directly from your emails. You can also synchronize tasks between Smartsheet and Outlook to stay organized across both platforms.

9.2 Integration with Google Workspace

Smartsheet seamlessly integrates with Google Workspace (formerly G Suite), enabling you to collaborate and manage projects more effectively using Google's suite of productivity tools. Here's how to integrate Smartsheet with Google Workspace:

Google Sheets Integration: Import data from Google Sheets into Smartsheet or export Smartsheet data to Google Sheets for further analysis. Create live connections between Smartsheet and Google Sheets to keep data synced in real-time.

Google Drive Integration: Attach files and documents from Google Drive directly to your Smartsheet rows for easy access and collaboration. You can also link Google Drive folders to Smartsheet to centralize document management.

Google Calendar Integration: Sync tasks and project milestones from Smartsheet to Google Calendar to visualize project schedules and deadlines alongside your other commitments.

9.3 Integration with Third-Party Apps
Smartsheet offers a wide range of integrations with third-party apps and services, allowing you to extend its

functionality and connect with your favorite tools. Here are some popular third-party integrations:

Zapier: Use Zapier to automate workflows and connect Smartsheet with thousands of other apps and services, such as Slack, Trello, Salesforce, and more. Create custom automation workflows without writing any code.

Microsoft Power Automate: Formerly known as Microsoft Flow, Power Automate allows you to automate tasks and processes between Smartsheet and Microsoft 365 applications, as well as other third-party services.

Jira: Integrate Smartsheet with Jira to synchronize project tasks, issues, and updates between the two platforms. Streamline collaboration between project management and software development teams.

9.4 Setting Up Integrations

To set up integrations in Smartsheet, follow these general steps:

Access Integrations: Explore the "Apps & Integrations" section in Smartsheet or visit the respective marketplace for the tool you want to integrate with.
Choose Integration: Select the integration you want to set up

and follow the instructions to connect your Smartsheet account with the external tool.

Authorize Access: Grant permissions to allow the integration to access your Smartsheet data and perform the necessary actions.

Configure Settings: Customize the integration settings according to your preferences, such as specifying data mappings, scheduling automated actions, and defining triggers.

Test Integration: Test the integration to ensure that data is syncing correctly and that the desired actions are being performed as expected.

By integrating Smartsheet with other tools, you can streamline your workflows, centralize data management, and collaborate more effectively with your team members. In the next chapter, we'll explore how to track progress and performance in Smartsheet using dashboards and reports.

Chapter 10: Tracking Progress with Dashboards and Reports

In this chapter, we'll dive into how to track progress and performance in Smartsheet using dashboards and reports, enabling you to visualize data, gain insights, and make informed decisions.

10.1 Understanding Dashboards

Dashboards in Smartsheet provide a centralized hub for monitoring key metrics, project statuses, and performance indicators in real-time. Here's how to create and utilize dashboards effectively:

Creating a Dashboard: To create a dashboard, navigate to the "Dashboards" tab in Smartsheet and click on the "Create Dashboard" button. Give your dashboard a descriptive name and choose the appropriate sharing settings.

Adding Widgets: Widgets are components that display specific data or visualizations on your dashboard. You can add widgets such as charts, grids, metrics, and web content to your dashboard by clicking on the "Add Widget" button.

Customizing Layout: Arrange widgets on your dashboard to create a layout that suits your preferences and highlights the most important information. You can resize, move, and group widgets to organize your dashboard effectively.

Configuring Widget Settings: Customize the settings of each widget to specify the data source, visualization type, filters, and other options. This allows you to tailor the widgets to display the data and insights you need.

10.2 Creating Reports

Reports in Smartsheet enable you to aggregate and summarize data from multiple sheets, providing a comprehensive view of project progress and performance. Here's how to create and utilize reports:

Creating a Report: To create a report, navigate to the "Reports" tab in Smartsheet and click on the "Create Report" button. Choose the sheets you want to include in the report and define the columns you want to display.

Customizing Settings: Customize the settings of your report, such as grouping options, sorting criteria, summary fields, and filters. This allows you to organize and present the data in the report effectively.

Reviewing Results: Once your report is created, review the data and insights presented in the report to ensure they align with your project objectives and requirements. Make any necessary adjustments to the report settings or data sources as needed.

Sharing and Collaboration: Share your reports with team members, stakeholders, and clients to keep them informed about project progress and performance. You can also schedule automatic updates to ensure that the report data is always up-to-date.

10.3 Utilizing Metrics and KPIs

Metrics and Key Performance Indicators (KPIs) help you track the performance of your projects and ensure that you're meeting your goals and objectives. Here's how to utilize metrics and KPIs effectively:

Identifying Key Metrics: Determine the key metrics and KPIs that are most relevant to your project objectives. These could include metrics such as task completion rate, project milestones achieved, budget variance, and more.

Creating Metrics Widgets: Use widgets such as charts and metrics on your dashboard to visualize key metrics and KPIs in real-time. This allows you to monitor project performance at a glance and quickly identify areas that require attention.

Setting Targets and Benchmarks: Establish targets and benchmarks for each key metric to track progress and performance against predefined goals. This helps you stay focused on achieving your project objectives and allows you to make data-driven decisions.
Analyzing Trends and Patterns: Use reports to analyze trends and patterns in your project data over time. Identify areas of

improvement, track changes in performance, and make adjustments to your project strategy as needed based on insights gained from the data.

By utilizing dashboards, reports, metrics, and KPIs effectively, you can track progress, monitor performance, and make informed decisions to ensure the success of your projects in Smartsheet. In the next chapter, we'll explore how to streamline communication and collaboration with Smartsheet forms and automation.

Chapter 11: Streamlining Communication and Collaboration with Smartsheet Forms and Automation

In this chapter, we'll explore how to streamline communication and collaboration in Smartsheet using forms and automation. Forms allow you to collect structured data from collaborators, while automation helps automate repetitive tasks and workflows.

11.1 Creating Smartsheet Forms

Smartsheet forms provide an easy way to gather information from team members, clients, and stakeholders in a structured format. Here's how to create and utilize Smartsheet forms effectively:

Accessing Form Builder: Navigate to the sheet for which you want to create a form. Click on the "Forms" tab in the toolbar and select "Edit Form" to access the form builder.

Designing the Form: Use the form builder to design your form by adding fields such as text fields, dropdowns, checkboxes, and attachments. Customize the field labels and options to match the information you need to collect.

Setting Form Options: Configure form settings such as form name, description, and confirmation message. You can also enable notifications to receive email alerts whenever a form submission is received.

Sharing the Form: Once your form is ready, share it with your team members, clients, or stakeholders by copying the form URL or embedding it on a website. You can also generate a QR code for easy access to the form.

Collecting Responses: As responses are submitted through the form, they are automatically captured and added as new rows in the associated Smartsheet. You can view and manage form responses directly within the sheet.

11.2 Automating Workflows with Form Submissions

Automating workflows with form submissions allows you to trigger actions and notifications based on the data collected through Smartsheet forms. Here's how to set up automation with form submissions:

Accessing Automation Settings: In the sheet containing your form responses, click on the "Automation" tab in the toolbar and select "Manage Automations" to access automation settings.

Creating an Automation Rule: Click on the "New Automation" button to create a new automation rule. Choose "Form Submitted" as the trigger event.

Defining Conditions (Optional): Optionally, you can define conditions that must be met for the automation rule to be triggered. For example, you may want to trigger an action only when specific form fields are filled out.

Configuring Actions: Choose the actions you want to perform when a form submission is received. Actions can include sending email notifications, updating cells, creating new rows or tasks, and more.

Testing and Activating Automation: Test the automation rule to ensure it works as expected. Once satisfied, activate the automation rule to start automating workflows with form submissions.

11.3 Use Cases for Forms and Automation

Forms and automation can be used in various scenarios to streamline communication and collaboration. Here are some common use cases:

Task Assignment: Use forms to collect task requests from team members and automatically assign tasks to the appropriate individuals based on the submitted information.

Issue Tracking: Create a form for reporting issues or bugs, and set up automation to notify the relevant team members and track the status of issue resolution.

Feedback Collection: Gather feedback from clients or stakeholders using a form, and automate notifications to the relevant teams for review and action.

Event Registration: Create a form for event registration, and automate the creation of attendee lists, sending confirmations, and updating event details.

Resource Requests: Allow team members to request resources or equipment through a form, and automate the procurement process based on the submitted requests.

By leveraging Smartsheet forms and automation, you can streamline communication, automate workflows, and improve collaboration across your projects and teams. In the next chapter, we'll explore best practices for managing permissions and security in Smartsheet.

Chapter 12: Managing Permissions and Security in Smartsheet

In this chapter, we'll explore best practices for managing permissions and ensuring security in Smartsheet, allowing you to control access to your data and protect sensitive information effectively.

12.1 Understanding Permissions in Smartsheet

Permissions in Smartsheet determine who can view, edit, and manage your sheets, reports, and other assets. Here's an overview of the key permission levels:

Admin: Admins have full control over the account settings, including user management, sharing settings, and account billing. They can also access and modify all sheets and reports within the account.

Editor: Editors can view, edit, and manage sheets and reports. They can make changes to data, formatting, and sharing settings within the sheets they have access to.

Viewer: Viewers can only view and interact with sheets and reports. They cannot make changes to the data or sharing settings. They may also have limited functionality, depending on the permissions granted by the sheet owner.

Reviewer: Reviewers have similar permissions to viewers but may have additional capabilities, such as the ability to leave comments and make suggestions.

12.2 Setting Permissions for Sheets and Reports

Here's how to manage permissions for sheets and reports in Smartsheet:

Access Sharing Settings: Open the sheet or report you want to manage permissions for and click on the "Share" button in the toolbar.

Add Collaborators: Enter the email addresses of the individuals or groups you want to share the sheet or report with. Specify their permission level (Editor, Viewer, etc.) and customize additional sharing settings as needed.

Set Up Sharing Options: Choose whether to share the sheet or report with specific individuals, groups, or entire domains. You can also set permissions for specific rows, columns, or cells if needed.

Review Permissions: Review the list of collaborators and their respective permission levels to ensure that the sharing settings meet your requirements. Make any necessary adjustments before finalizing the sharing settings.

12.3 Using Workspace Permissions

Workspaces in Smartsheet allow you to organize and manage related sheets and reports more efficiently. Here's how to manage permissions for workspaces:

Create a Workspace: Create a new workspace or access an existing workspace where you want to manage permissions.

Access Workspace Settings: Click on the settings icon next to the workspace name and select "Workspace settings" to access the workspace settings.

Manage Members: In the workspace settings, you can add or remove members and set their permission levels for the workspace. You can also customize additional settings such as workspace description and sharing options.

Review and Adjust Permissions: Review the list of workspace members and their respective permissions. Make any necessary adjustments to ensure that only authorized individuals have access to the workspace and its contents.

12.4 Best Practices for Security and Data Protection

To ensure security and data protection in Smartsheet, consider implementing the following best practices:

Regularly Review Permissions: Periodically review and update permissions for sheets, reports, and workspaces to ensure that only authorized individuals have access to sensitive information.

Use Strong Passwords: Encourage users to use strong, unique passwords for their Smartsheet accounts to prevent unauthorized access.

Enable Two-Factor Authentication (2FA): Enable two-factor authentication for added security, requiring users to provide a second form of verification in addition to their password when logging in.

Educate Users: Educate users about security best practices, such as avoiding sharing sensitive information through unsecured channels and being cautious of phishing attempts.

Monitor Activity Logs: Regularly monitor activity logs to track user actions and detect any suspicious activity or unauthorized access.

By following these best practices, you can effectively manage permissions and ensure the security of your data in Smartsheet. In the next chapter, we'll explore how to optimize performance and scalability in Smartsheet for large-scale projects and organizations.

Chapter 13: Optimizing Performance and Scalability in Smartsheet

In this chapter, we'll delve into strategies for optimizing performance and scalability in Smartsheet, ensuring smooth operation and efficiency, even with large-scale projects and organizations.

13.1 Efficient Sheet Design

Efficient sheet design plays a crucial role in optimizing performance in Smartsheet. Here are some tips for designing efficient sheets:

Limit Columns and Rows: Avoid excessive use of columns and rows in your sheets, as this can slow down performance. Remove any unnecessary columns or rows to keep your sheets lean and efficient.

Use Filters and Views: Utilize filters and views to focus on relevant data and reduce the amount of information displayed on the sheet at any given time. This can help improve loading times and responsiveness.

Minimize Cell References: Limit the use of cross-sheet cell references, as excessive references can impact performance. Instead, consider consolidating related data into a single sheet or using formulas to calculate values directly within the same sheet.

13.2 Utilizing Reports and Dashboards

Reports and dashboards provide a consolidated view of project data and key metrics, improving visibility and decision-making. Here's how to optimize reports and dashboards for performance:

Aggregate Data Thoughtfully: When creating reports, aggregate data thoughtfully to minimize the number of rows and columns being processed. Use summary fields and groupings to organize data hierarchically and avoid overwhelming the system with excessive data.

Limit Widget Count: Avoid overloading dashboards with too many widgets, as this can slow down loading times. Focus on displaying the most relevant information and consider organizing widgets into tabs or sections for better organization.

13.3 Managing Attachments and Comments

Attachments and comments can impact sheet performance, especially in sheets with large amounts of data. Here's how to manage attachments and comments effectively:

Archive Old Attachments: Regularly review and archive old attachments to prevent them from cluttering the sheet and slowing down performance. Consider storing archived attachments in a separate location or using external storage solutions.

Limit Comment Threads: Encourage users to keep comment threads concise and relevant to avoid excessive clutter. Consider archiving or deleting outdated comments to keep the sheet organized and responsive.

13.4 Monitoring and Optimization

Regular monitoring and optimization are essential for maintaining optimal performance in Smartsheet. Here are some best practices for monitoring and optimization:

Monitor System Performance: Use Smartsheet's performance monitoring tools to track system performance and identify potential bottlenecks or areas for improvement.

Regular Maintenance: Schedule regular maintenance tasks, such as archiving old data, optimizing sheet designs, and reviewing sharing settings, to keep your Smartsheet environment running smoothly.

Stay Informed: Stay informed about Smartsheet updates and new features that may improve performance or introduce optimization opportunities. Take advantage of training resources and support channels to stay up-to-date with best practices.

13.5 Scaling for Growth

As your organization grows, it's essential to scale your Smartsheet implementation accordingly. Here are some tips for scaling Smartsheet for growth:

Evaluate Workflows: Regularly evaluate your workflows and processes to identify areas for optimization and automation. Streamline processes and automate repetitive tasks to improve efficiency and scalability.

Train Users: Provide ongoing training and support to users to ensure they are proficient in using Smartsheet effectively. Encourage adoption of best practices and optimization techniques to maximize productivity and scalability.

Leverage Enterprise Features: If your organization requires advanced functionality or customization, consider leveraging Smartsheet's enterprise features and integrations to meet your specific needs.

By implementing these strategies for optimizing performance and scalability in Smartsheet, you can ensure that your organization can effectively manage large-scale projects and operations while maintaining efficiency and responsiveness. In the next chapter, we'll explore advanced customization options and integrations in Smartsheet for tailored solutions.

Chapter 14: Advanced Customization and Integrations in Smartsheet

In this chapter, we'll explore advanced customization options and integrations in Smartsheet, empowering users to tailor the platform to their specific needs and integrate it seamlessly with other tools and systems.

14.1 Customizing Sheet Templates

Customizing sheet templates allows you to create standardized formats for various types of projects and workflows. Here's how to customize sheet templates effectively:

Identify Requirements: Determine the specific requirements and features needed for your template, such as columns, formulas, conditional formatting, and attachments.

Design Template: Create a new sheet and customize it according to your requirements. Add and format columns, set up formulas, apply conditional formatting, and insert any necessary attachments or comments.

Save as Template: Once your sheet is customized, save it as a template by clicking on the "File" menu, selecting "Save as

Template," and providing a descriptive name and description for the template.

Share Template: Share the template with your team members or save it to the organizational template library for easy access by other users.

14.2 Building Custom Reports and Dashboards

Custom reports and dashboards allow you to present data and insights in a visually appealing and informative manner. Here's how to build custom reports and dashboards:

Define Objectives: Determine the key metrics and insights you want to showcase in your report or dashboard. Consider the audience and their specific needs and preferences.

Select Data Sources: Choose the appropriate data sources, such as sheets, reports, or external databases, to include in your report or dashboard. Ensure that the data is accurate, relevant, and up-to-date.

Design Layout: Design the layout of your report or dashboard by selecting appropriate widgets and arranging them to convey information effectively. Use charts, graphs, metrics, and text widgets to present data in a visually appealing format.

Customize Appearance: Customize the appearance of your report or dashboard by applying themes, colors, and branding elements to match your organization's visual identity.

14.3 Integrating with External Systems

Integrating Smartsheet with external systems allows you to streamline workflows, automate tasks, and centralize data management. Here's how to integrate Smartsheet with external systems:

Explore Integration Options: Identify the external systems and tools you want to integrate with Smartsheet, such as CRM systems, project management tools, or accounting software.

Select Integration Method: Choose the appropriate integration method based on the capabilities of the external system and your specific requirements. Options may include API integrations, pre-built connectors, or third-party integration platforms.

Configure Integration: Configure the integration by specifying data mappings, authentication settings, and synchronization options. Test the integration to ensure that data is syncing accurately between Smartsheet and the external system. Automate Workflows: Once the integration is set up, automate workflows and tasks to streamline processes and ensure data consistency across systems. Trigger actions and notifications based on data changes or predefined events.

14.4 Leveraging Smartsheet Add-Ons and Solutions

Smartsheet offers a wide range of add-ons and solutions developed by third-party vendors and partners. Here's how to leverage Smartsheet add-ons and solutions:

Explore Marketplace: Explore the Smartsheet Marketplace to discover add-ons and solutions that extend the functionality of Smartsheet and address specific use cases or industry needs.

Evaluate Options: Evaluate different add-ons and solutions based on their features, user reviews, and compatibility with your existing workflows and systems.

Install and Configure: Install the selected add-ons or solutions and configure them according to your requirements. Follow the provided instructions for setup and customization.

Integrate with Workflows: Integrate the add-ons or solutions seamlessly into your existing workflows and processes. Leverage automation features to trigger actions and events based on interactions with the add-ons.

By mastering advanced customization options and integrations in Smartsheet, you can create tailored solutions that meet the unique needs of your organization and enhance productivity and collaboration across teams. In the next chapter, we'll explore strategies for continuous improvement and innovation in Smartsheet usage.

Chapter 15: Strategies for Continuous Improvement and Innovation in Smartsheet Usage

In this final chapter, we'll discuss strategies for continuously improving and innovating in your usage of Smartsheet. By embracing ongoing learning, optimization, and innovation, you can maximize the benefits of Smartsheet for your projects and workflows.

15.1 Embrace Lifelong Learning

Continuous learning is key to staying informed about new features, best practices, and advanced techniques in Smartsheet. Here's how to embrace lifelong learning:

Stay Updated: Regularly explore Smartsheet's official documentation, blogs, webinars, and training resources to stay updated on new features, tips, and tricks.

Community Engagement: Join the Smartsheet Community to connect with other users, share experiences, and learn from each other's successes and challenges.

Certification Programs: Consider participating in Smartsheet certification programs to validate your skills, expand your knowledge, and enhance your credibility as a Smartsheet expert.

15.2 Solicit Feedback and Iterate

Feedback from users and stakeholders is invaluable for identifying areas for improvement and driving innovation. Here's how to solicit feedback and iterate on your Smartsheet usage:

Feedback Channels: Create channels for collecting feedback from users, stakeholders, and team members. Encourage open communication and provide opportunities for feedback through surveys, meetings, and discussion forums.

Iterative Improvement: Use feedback received to identify pain points, address user needs, and make iterative improvements to your Smartsheet setup, workflows, and processes.

User Testing: Conduct user testing and usability studies to gather insights into how users interact with Smartsheet and identify opportunities for enhancing usability and user experience.

15.3 Explore Advanced Features and Integrations

Continuously explore advanced features and integrations in Smartsheet to unlock new capabilities and streamline workflows. Here's how to explore advanced features and integrations:

Experimentation: Experiment with advanced features such as formulas, automation, integrations, and API capabilities to discover new ways of leveraging Smartsheet for your projects and workflows.

Pilot Projects: Launch pilot projects to test out new features, integrations, or workflows in a controlled environment before rolling them out organization-wide.

Collaboration with IT: Collaborate with your organization's IT department to explore integration opportunities with other systems and tools used across the organization.

15.4 Foster a Culture of Innovation

Fostering a culture of innovation within your organization encourages creativity, experimentation, and continuous improvement. Here's how to foster a culture of innovation:

Leadership Support: Secure support from organizational leadership to prioritize innovation and allocate resources for experimentation and exploration.

Recognition and Rewards: Recognize and reward individuals and teams for innovative ideas, successful experiments, and impactful improvements in Smartsheet usage.

Cross-Functional Collaboration: Encourage cross-functional collaboration and knowledge sharing to facilitate the exchange of ideas and best practices across teams and departments.

15.5 Measure Success and Iterate

Measuring success and iterating based on insights gained is essential for driving continuous improvement in Smartsheet usage. Here's how to measure success and iterate:

Define Key Metrics: Define key performance indicators (KPIs) and success metrics related to Smartsheet usage, such as project completion rates, time savings, and user satisfaction scores.

Track Progress: Regularly track and analyze performance against the defined metrics to identify areas of success and opportunities for improvement.

Iterate and Adapt: Based on the insights gained from performance metrics and user feedback, iterate on your

Smartsheet setup, workflows, and processes to optimize performance and drive ongoing improvement.

By embracing strategies for continuous improvement and innovation in Smartsheet usage, you can adapt to evolving needs, drive efficiency, and unlock new possibilities for collaboration and productivity in your organization. With a commitment to lifelong learning, feedback-driven iteration, and a culture of innovation, you can maximize the value of Smartsheet for your projects and workflows.

Made in the USA
Las Vegas, NV
19 October 2024

97057266R00037